She DOESN'T HATE POLYGAMY, *You* SHOULDN'T TOO

ALLI UMIH

Published by:

Unit No. E-10-5, Jalan SS 15/4G, Subang Square,
47500 Subang Jaya, Selangor, Malaysia
+603-5612-2407 (office) / +6017-399-7411 (mobile)
info@tertib.press
www.tertib.press
@tertibpress (Facebook & Instagram)

Author	:	Alli Umih
Editor	:	Norashikin Azizan
Cover design	:	Abdul Adzim Md Daim
Book design	:	Abdul Adzim Md Daim

SHE DOESN'T HATE POLYGAMY, YOU SHOULDN'T TOO

First Edition: August 2022

Perpustakaan Negara Malaysia   Cataloguing-in-Publication Data

Alli Umih
She DOESN'T HATE POLYGAMY, You SHOULDN'T TOO /
Author : Alli Umih.
ISBN 978-967-2844-09-9
1. Polygamy--Religious aspects--Islam.
2. Marriage--Religious aspects--Islam.
3. Polygamy (Islamic law).
I. Title.
297.577

CONTENTS

This book is dedicated to every Muslim woman,
striving every day to please Allah s.w.t.

INTRODUCTION

I was born into a polygamous home, I grew up in a polygamous community, I am descended from a line of polygamists (from both my maternal and paternal branch of the family), and as soon as I understood the concept of marriage, I vowed never to be in a polygamous marriage.

I saw my mother's tears, I heard about my grandma's pains and caught glimpses of my neighbour's suffering.

No, never, no way! I will not go down that road.

My sisters and I did not make a formal pact to escape polygamy, but after all the dramas of family life we were exposed to, I know we all privately abhorred the system and could not wait to get out of it. With a family that was mostly female (my dad had eight girls and a boy from four wives), the causes for quarrels were limitless.

Alḥamdulillāh, my father advocated education for girls, so obtaining a university-level education was our first ticket to freedom from the polygamous system. Freedom from squabbling siblings, bickering wives, and the occasional husband fights.

My five sisters before me started the tradition of leaving for university with almost all of our belongings and only visiting home during rare occasions (probably for Eid celebrations and to collect provisions for school).

The second ticket was to nab a Christian guy before graduation, waltz a tale to my father about how we were deeply in love, and convince him how the guy would so lovingly support our religious choices. My father would agree, there would be a wedding, and bam, three months later my sisters go by a western-edited name: Alima becomes Annie, Maimuna becomes Amanda. And unfortunately, they drift off away from Islam. But *alḥamdulillāh*, I took a pass from the second ticket tradition.

And no, it was not as a result of my love for Islam or my love for Allah s.w.t., rather it was His love for me. His mercy guided me during my university days to seek the "real Islam", and His grace helped me practise the truth when I found it. So, no Christian guy-nabbing for me.

Fast-forward two decades, I am writing a book entitled: *She Doesn't Hate Polygamy, You Shouldn't Too.*

You see, humans generally have this natural tendency to want, and then when they get it, they become reluctant to share. I also have this desire, so do not let this sentence, "She doesn't hate polygamy" make you hate me or throw out the book.

Life is a test from Allah s.w.t. to see how willingly we let go of our desires to please Him. If we are pleased with Allah s.w.t. as our Creator, and the Prophet s.a.w as our

Messenger, shouldn't we then accept Allah's words and force our *nafs* (desire) to adhere to every bit of it?

Allah s.w.t. made it easy for me after lots of *du'a'* (supplication). Not because I had no other choice, or because I wanted to justify my *iman* (faith) to the world, but because I wanted Allah's words to be the most beloved thing in my life. He answered my *du'a'*, and may He answer yours too.

Chapter One:

THE QUR'AN IS MY COMPANION

Alhamdulillāh, after marriage, Allah s.w.t. blessed me with two kids; a son and a daughter. It was when I was pregnant with my third baby—three months along; when Allah s.w.t. tried me with polygamy. I am certain it is from Allah s.w.t., because certainly, everything revolves by the command of Allah s.w.t.

I never saw my spouse as polygamous, in fact, I had felt confident in his "monogamous-ness" considering he is descended from a line of monogamous marriages, on both sides of his family.

The news made me feel horrible and depressed. Combining the wretchedness of morning sickness and the bomb of polygamy, the consequences almost did me in. During the first and second trimester of my pregnancy, I was hospitalised thrice, suffering from severe dehydration and depression.

You must think, "Oh! What a pity." "I'm sure the spouse called it off." These might be your thoughts… Wrong! He went ahead with the preparations, the travelling, shopping, everything. Yeah, he got married in my seventh month of pregnancy.

Subḥanallāh, how come I am still alive?

Well, I would answer with, "*Alḥamdulillāh*, I had Allah s.w.t., and I had His words, the Qur'an."

At first, I called my mother, sobbing, hoping for some ease. She was heartbroken. She had hoped none of her kids would have to go through polygamy. My elder sisters were "safely" married to Christians. She gave me the "It's a man thing" speech. She could not tell me what I wanted to hear, or even what I needed to hear.

Then I surfed the web, seeking articles or lectures that could help me understand this situation, and deal with it.

Alḥamdulillāh, I found many resources online, loads of videos and audio lectures on dealing with depression and understanding life's challenges. I also found many books on related subjects.

But, other than a couple of articles on polygamy, I failed to find a book or lecture on practically dealing with polygamy authored by a woman.

Well permit me to be sexist here, but a male author would never be able to touch on understanding and dealing with polygamy from a woman's point of view.

Those resources took me far, but the pain in the hole of my heart could not be filled except with the Qur'an.

I swear by Allah, that the answers we seek are in the Qur'an. If you have not found it, it is either because you have not searched for it, or you do not really believe in your heart that you can find it in the Qur'an.

The Qur'an had always been my companion, and in those trying days, it came to my rescue.

The verse "Allah will never burden a soul more than it can bear" in *Suratul Baqarah*, kept resonating in my head, so I knew I could handle this test Allah s.w.t. tried me with.

For every fear that I had, every question I pondered on, I was inspired by the verses from the Qur'an.

I turned to Allah s.w.t. in *taḥajjud* (night prayer), I could not fast because of my pregnant condition, so I was making *du'a'* fervently.

Practically, I started with *Surah Yusuf*. There is a ton of treasure in that *surah* (chapter) for the hurting heart, especially if the hurt is from family. The English translation gave me relief, and its *tafsir* (exegesis) certified my relief.

Whether I was in the wrong or right in my hurting, *Surah Yusuf* calmed me, it assured me of Allah's knowledge of my feelings and promised me retribution for the wrongs I was facing at that point (which I later realised that there had been no wrongs), and it stopped the bleeding in my broken heart.

For practicality, allow me to highlight my conversations with Allah s.w.t. through the Qur'an:

- When I felt betrayed by my spouse's actions was because we had a joint business, a joint account and I had always thought that we had the same goals (there was definitely no 'Item 4: Another wife' on my list); Allah s.w.t. consoled me that the act of supporting my spouse will be rewarded.

"...indeed, he who fears Allah and is patient, then indeed, Allah does not allow to be lost the reward of those who do good."

(Yusuf, 12:90)

- When I despised myself for living my past years for my spouse's approval instead of Allah's. He promised me forgiveness.

"Say, 'O' My servants who have transgressed against themselves [by sinning], do not despair of the mercy of Allah. Indeed, Allah forgives all sins. Indeed, it is He who is the Forgiving, the Merciful.'"

(az-Zumar, 39:53)

- He quelled my urge to complain to the world about my spouse's actions with Prophet Ya'qub's a.s statement,

"He said, 'I only complain of my suffering and my grief to Allah, and I know from Allah that which you do not know.'"

(Yusuf, 12:86)

- He reminded me that He alone provides for His creatures, the addition to the family does not affect my family's sustenance. It is from Him I should ask.

"And there is no creature on earth but that upon Allah is its provision, and He knows its place of dwelling and place of storage. All is in a clear register."

(Hud, 11:6)

- He redirected my heart to Him. Reminding me that my life should not be about competing for spousal love, but rather it should be about competing for His pleasure.

"[He] who created death and life to test you [as to] which of you is best in deed (to do them only for Allah's sake)—and He is the Exalted in Might, the Forgiving"

(al-Mulk, 67:2)

● And when all I wanted was a divorce—I even had fantasies about how a bearded knight would swoop in for me and my kids, Allah reminded me that the reward of the hereafter was the best.

"But those who had been given knowledge said, 'Woe to you! The reward of Allah is better for he who believes and does righteousness. And none are granted it except the patient.'"

(al-Qaṣaṣ, 28:80)

● He sent this Qur'an with its stories as a mercy, a reminder for His creatures who believe.

"There was certainly in their stories a lesson for those of understanding. Never was it [i.e., the Qur'an] a narration invented, but a confirmation of what was before it and a detailed explanation of all things and guidance and mercy for a people who believe."

(Yusuf, 12:111)

Chapter Two:

THERE IS NOTHING WRONG WITH YOU

One thing polygamy does to almost every woman is, question her sense of self. "Am I not pretty enough?" "Am I not supportive enough?" "Is my cooking not good enough?" Unending questions of self-doubt.

If you are on this bus ride, you should stop, alight, and ask for a refund.

I could tell you, "You are a beautiful perfect soul", but I would not! No one is perfect, not the other wife, and not even your spouse.

We all are imperfect, striving to reach Allah's mercy—the worthy destination, with our different life scripts.

Your spouse's decision to take another wife has nothing to do with you or your perceived shortcomings. Despite what your spouse, family or friends may say, it is not your childlessness, your inability to give birth to a son after the fifth girl, or the lack of a daughter in your family that is making your spouse consider another wife.

Neither is it your dark skin, nor your small stature.

I swear by Allah s.w.t., I swear by Allah s.w.t., and I swear by Allah s.w.t., nothing touches any creation, except what has been destined for it. These are not my words but the words of your Creator.

"No disaster strikes upon the earth or among yourselves except that it is in a register before We bring it into being—indeed that, for Allah is easy."

In order that you not despair over what has eluded you and not exult [in pride] over what He has given you. And Allah does not like everyone self-deluded and boastful."

(al-Hadid, 57:22-23)

Allah s.w.t. tells us that it is not solely by our efforts we keep our marriages. All matters return to Him. And He warns us from feeling boastful, thinking that it is because we are better homemakers that our marriages thrive, unlike others, whom we think we are better than.

A woman could be a lazy and uncaring wife, and you find her spouse patient, covering her faults. Another woman who is better could have a critiquing spouse. This is all from the Qadar of Allah s.w.t.

We all have good days and "other" days. On some days, you take time to prim, so you look fabulous, the meals are delicious, and the house is sparkling clean. On these "other" days, you just want to get the basic house chores done and take a break.

Whatever you choose to do, as long as you are in obedience to Allah s.w.t., and you are giving your best (not the other wife's best), then you are who you should be. Do not ever belittle yourself or your achievements based on this. If there are areas in your life that need improving, get to them because you have to and never let this be your new deciding factor.

Let's say that the new wife is a fitness guru, then bam, you chuck your carbs, and start chugging green smoothies. You are then definitely going into ogre-mode with self-loathing if the carb-withdrawals do not do you in first!

Or she is a *hafidha* (Qur'an memoriser), and you suddenly start memorising the Qur'an.

These are good actions by themselves, but because you are doing it to be like someone else, you lose the blessings and earn no reward.

And except for situations where the other wife is someone you already know; I cannot understand why you should know anything personal about her.

Your husband starting another family has nothing to do with you, so do not concern yourself with what Allah s.w.t.

has shielded you from. There is no verse or ḥadith obligating you to co-wives, other than the obligation of the Islamic sisterhood. You have a right to separate dwellings so take advantage of it because witnessing the lovey-dovey of the newlyweds might make you resentful. Please save yourself from the heartache.

As a people-pleaser, I always bend myself backwards, trying to stay true to the label. I also do not take well with failing or criticism. One sign of dissatisfaction with myself sends me into depression. So, imagine how it feels like, trying to cope with this 'dissatisfaction' with my services and the need for my customer (spouse) to seek satisfaction elsewhere. I felt terribly insufficient.

But *alhamdulillāh* for the gift of this trial. I had to go for counselling to deal with my depression, and this helped me address the underlying problem of people-pleasing that was eating away my self-esteem. It was not my duty to conform to either my spouse's wife model or society's. Allah is The Sufficient, and He does not expect that of me.

Over time, civilisations and cultures, Allah s.w.t. has given us a never-changing model that, I will conform to. I had to go back to the book of Allah s.w.t. and the *sunnah* (traditions of the Prophet s.a.w.) to understand what Allah s.w.t. expects of us in our dealings with His other creatures.

I had to gradually learn (I am still learning), how to be the person Allah s.w.t. created me to be. Let me highlight what I mean:

- My spouse is a gift from Allah s.w.t., I should of course love and honour him, but I should not make him the essence of my existence. Allah's pleasure should always be my goal foremost.

- People's pleasure or anger should not be a cause for my joy or depression. Pleasing Allah s.w.t. should be enough for me.

- If I had to do any deed or overlook any slight mistake, it should be only to seek the pleasure of Allah s.w.t. alone and not people's accolades.

- And as long as I am trying my best to conform to Allah's model of a Muslim woman, then I am okay as I am.

Chapter Three:

IT IS OKAY TO DISLIKE IT

Oftentimes, people confuse the use of a headscarf with piety, the use of a hijab with perfection, and when you decide to use the niqab, aha! You now roll with the angels, *astaghfirullāh*.

My obedience to Allah s.w.t. in how I dress does not change my being as a human. I still have my human desires, which I fight daily, and *shaytan* (devil) still comes to divert me from the straight path with every chance he gets.

People have these expectations of us, but we also stress ourselves trying to conform to them.

It is okay to dislike polygamy. It is okay to feel betrayed by your spouse. It is okay to feel sad about the situation. It is okay to feel hurt. It is okay to cry. These feelings are all okay, it makes you human.

But note that I wrote, "feel". Those feelings will come, even Allah s.w.t., your Creator confirms this.

"...but perhaps you hate a thing and it is good for you; and perhaps you love a thing and it is bad for you. And Allah knows, while you know not."

(al-Baqarah, 2:216)

But it is how you react to those feelings that determine your state with Allah s.w.t. You could go bat-crazy on your spouse, troll the lady on social networks, wail to everyone who will listen about all the wrongs, or you could go back to Allah s.w.t., to the *sunnah*, and know Allah's expectations of you.

I had a lot of negative feelings (not being related in any way to bats), but *alhamdulillāh*, there was no craziness. I curbed them, sorted them, and found my silver linings in the dark cloud.

I like to think that what a battle is to Muslim men equals what polygamy is to Muslim women. They are both disliked, but there is good in them. If Allah s.w.t. permits polygamy, then there must be goodness in it. So, I forced my *nafs* to let go of the ill feelings as I sourced for all the good that I could milk from the situation.

Here is my list of "goods":

- Remembering my "people-pleasing-ness", I found myself most times bending to my spouse's decisions, in all matters, even trivial ones like meals, entertainment, and clothing. Polygamy kind of got him out of my radar to allow me to find myself. The days he was gone, were my coolest (he is not supposed to see this). I am the boss of my home! There is no pressure to clean, cook a big meal, primp and polish (my spouse is very traditional).

On those blessed days, the ratty PJs come out, there is take out from that new place I have been yearning to try, and the kids love this non-yelling me (yeah, on these auspicious days, the Legos can run wild all over the floor).

- All the people I want to visit, and all those who want to visit me, I schedule for those days. Visitations are more fun without my spouse. I can ask for second helpings, laugh like a hyena, and take leftovers home without censure. All ḥalal fun, by the way.

- Then there are sleepovers; the kids and I love sleepovers. You should see me getting on the phone to get permission from my spouse to go to a relative's place for sleepovers. His days away equals sleepovers. Sleepovers equals having my host clean after me and my kids (I am not lazy, but I could do with breaks), which equals a more rested, happier me (wide grin). Perfect equation!

- Absence does make the heart fonder. Give me some days of frolicking, and I am looking forward to my spouse's return. I will start missing the sound of his voice, his footfalls, his everyday sounds.

You know your own unique situation. Write a list of every good thing you can get from this situation, and I tell you there are loads of good things, if, you only allow yourself to see them.

Remember the Prophet s.a.w. said:

"Unique are the affairs of every believer, for there is good for him in every situation, when good befalls him, he is grateful, and when he is tried, he is patient and that is better for him"

(Ṣaḥiḥ Muslim, Book 55 Ḥadith 82)

The reason you should write them is for when you forget. A situation may come at you where your thoughts and views become clouded by negative emotions. So, at times like these, you should consult your journal for a reminder.

Chapter Four:

ALLAH'S LEGISLATION IS ENOUGH REASON

When I initially tried to make sense of polygamy, I was given the "male to female ratio" reasoning. I got it from my mother, from my grandma, from my local Imam, and even from my spouse.

Albeit true, instead of soothing me, this reasoning brought on feelings of resentment and anger. I was so resentful that when my spouse wanted to explain away his "unfaithfulness" with this cliché reasoning, it made me angry at the statistics. Is it my fault if there are more women than men? Why must my spouse be the one to take in spouseless women? Must every woman get married?

These thoughts plagued my mind continuously, and as I tried to seek relief for my aching heart in resources addressing polygamy, I was also bombarded by this same reasoning, so I was furious.

When things we do not like happen to us, we mostly want closure, we want to understand it and see the sense in it before accepting it. The sense behind polygamy mostly peddled by Muslims and non-Muslims is this gender-based population rationale, and even though it is true, I could not find closure in it.

One of the gifts of being a Muslim is knowing Allah s.w.t., knowing His unique names and understanding what He created us for—to worship Him alone. Before this trial of polygamy, a piece of advice I always say to every Muslim I get a chance to talk to is, intend all your deeds for the sake of Allah s.w.t.

And this advice is what I believed kept me in that limbo, trying to come to terms with polygamy. And by Allah s.w.t., as soon as He guided me to it, I felt at peace.

We are human, and there is a bit of selfishness in us all, except by the mercy of Allah s.w.t., so please do not waltz the ratio, talk to me, or remind me of the ḥadith on loving one's brother (or in this case sister).

Anas ibn Malik reported: The Prophet s.a.w. said,

"None of you will have faith until he loves for his brother what he loves for himself."

(40 Ḥadith an-Nawawi, Ḥadith 13)

Do not tell me the single sister could be me, my daughter, my sister, or my aunt because I will throw a book at you. Instead, just tell me ***it is from the legislation of Allah s.w.t.*** (full stop).

That was the only reason that gave my heart rest, I was like, okay, so Allah s.w.t. legislated this, alright then, let me talk to Him. While I knew this already, it did not come to the forefront of my mind till later.

Nobody told me this reason, everyone wanted to tell me about how I was making a sacrifice for my spouse's peace, the sister's (new wife) joy, or helping to balance the population. As much as I care about making a positive change in this *dunya* (world), if my intention first is not for Allah s.w.t., then no, I am not going to do it. It will be a waste of my time, and I might even be punished.

I turned to the owner of hearts, I prayed "O' Allah, grant my heart rest," and *alḥamdulillāh*, He inspired me.

Allah s.w.t. is enough reason for me to accept polygamy.

This refocused me, it refocused my complaints, my *du'a'* and my expectations. Permit me to highlight these facts again:

- Allah s.w.t. loves me more than I can ever love myself, everything He created was for me; the solid straight roads for me to walk, the sun; serving my many needs. If He wants polygamy for me, then I will ask Him for the good from it and seek refuge in Him from the other parts. As it should be, my reliance should be on Allah s.w.t., so I should ask and expect only from Him (while doing the needful).

- Allah's pleasure should be our goal in every deed, so I will, by His mercy, uphold the rights of my spouse, and the other wife seeking only His pleasure, without expecting reciprocation.

- And because Allah s.w.t. has promised a great reward for every Muslim who hopes for the meeting with Him in the hereafter. So, if I am wronged, I will patiently seek justice, and hope for the reward with Allah s.w.t.

Chapter Five:

YOUR SPOUSE DID NOT SIN

This chapter will definitely have sisters scowling at me. Yes, most of the time the brothers go about taking on another wife in a shady way (they will tell you they wanted to spare your feelings). They will court the other wife, and sometimes conclude the *nikah* (solemnisation) process without you being any wiser.

There are the spouses who are empathic, they try to understand what you might be feeling, they even provide emotional support during the period (this one is a keeper, no matter the number of other wives, appreciate him), then there are the others (mostly the knowledgeable ones), they might want to tear your faith apart saying things like, "With your level of faith, how dare you feel sad!", or quoting the book of Ḥadith saying, "The Prophet Muḥammad s.a.w. never sought our mother Aisha r.a.'s consent before taking his other wives!", or even take the macho route, "I am the man, I don't need to consult you first!".

Well, I will say, whichever 'genre' of spouse you get, first know that:

- Your spouse did not commit a sin, he has the right to two, three, or four wives. It is not your business to question how he intends to care for them, nor how he plans to love them equally. Please fight against the urge to be a shrew, calling out to your spouse on all his

weaknesses because once you board the nagging bus you might never be able to alight. You will not find any peace on that ride; you will lose respect for yourself and lose a chance to be the better person Allah s.w.t. knows you can be.

- Another sincere reason for your concern might be your spouse's finances. You, as a good wife, might worry that your spouse will not be able to support multiple families. Tell your spouse your thoughts and stop there. Whether he agrees or disagrees, it should not give you sleepless nights. You have reminded him sincerely. Whether the reminder benefits is up to Allah s.w.t.

- Everyone to his or her deeds. And no deed even the size of a mustard seed goes unrewarded. So, if your spouse decides to empathise, he earns his reward, and if he decides to "macho-nise", he also earns something. You see, if we focus on Allah s.w.t. how we ought to, we will not see anything other than our relationship with Him. Polygamy can be a mercy to repair your relationship with Allah s.w.t. Allow your spouse to do his deeds, you do yours. To everyone their deeds.

- If you feel this intense love for your spouse, that the thought of him with another wife shatters your heart, please just ask Allah s.w.t. to help heal your heart. He knows best what you feel and only Him can give your heart rest. Ask Allah s.w.t. to cleanse your heart and fill it with love for only Him. Only love for Allah s.w.t. will bring you joy always, as love for creatures will always come to an end.

- Know your rights. We know we have waived most of our rights, choosing to be subservient wives. But why are we doing this? Is it to attain perfection in wifehood or to prevent your spouse from needing another wife? Or is it to seek the pleasure of Allah s.w.t.? If it is the latter, then know that there are rights Allah s.w.t. has given us as women. Read up on your rights and responsibilities and do the same for your husband too. The purpose of this is not to start a 'Retrieve-Our-Rights Campaign.' No, rather it is to arm you to better appreciate the limits Allah s.w.t. has set, out of His love for us.

Chapter Six:

DIVORCE IS NOT ALWAYS THE ANSWER

I would like to have someone answer me with a clear "Yes" or "No" to this question that I have asked myself several times in the past, and I still ask myself sometimes now.

If you were to search the internet for responses to this question, you would receive many results, which with each read, makes you more confused than the last.

No results tell you a plain and straight "Yes" or "No". You kick the ball, then you are dribbled with definitions, causative factors, statistics, advantages and disadvantages, and the ball is kicked back to you. The "Yes" or "No", is the ball in your court, you either shoot or save.

Let me tell you about my experience.

The search engine provided results from mostly well-meaning professionals. Factors to consider were explained and the cons and pros of divorce were highlighted with emphasis on marriages with children. *Alḥamdulillāh*, many useful resources are available online from great individuals, may Allah s.w.t. reward them all. They all had a common conclusion. After enlightening myself, it was up to me to consider my own special situation and the final response is mine to make.

At that time, I was not looking to do much thinking, I just wanted someone I could trust to tell me, "Pack your things and leave" or "Stay put!"

So, since the www did not decide for me, I visited the local Imam, and then counselling. I did not think I could thrive in a polygamy system, I wanted to leave and the only reason for my hesitation was the kids—would separating be what is best for them?

After my meeting with the Imam, and many counselling sessions, the ball was still in my court, waiting for a shoot or save.

I choose to save not because I looked at the statistics of behavioural patterns of kids from broken homes or the stigma of divorced Muslim women, *but* for the word of Allah s.w.t.

By Allah s.w.t., whoever wants to please Him, then He will guide his or her heart.

I was reminded of Allah's admonition to the Prophet Muhammad s.a.w. in *Suratul Tahrim:*

"O' Prophet, why do you prohibit [yourself from] what Allah has made lawful for you, seeking the approval of your wives? And Allah is Forgiving and Merciful." (at-Tahrim, 66:1)

You should read the *tafsir* of this verse for better understanding, but the summary was Allah s.w.t. admonishing the Prophet s.a.w. for forbidding a ḥalal drink for himself, just so he s.a.w. could please his wives. Imagine that.

It got me thinking, should I stop my spouse from what is ḥalal with threats that I will divorce him? And if I do that, what about my relationship with Allah s.w.t.?

I always believed I have been immensely blessed by Allah s.w.t. in every step of my life, I have always seen the love and care of Allah s.w.t. So, I wondered if I have said '*Alḥamdulillāh*' for Allah's decree that I have been pleased with and shouldn't I be patient with this decree that I disliked? And even if I wanted a divorce (which is not forbidden in Islam), how could I justify my reason to Allah s.w.t.? Is it because a servant (my spouse) obeys Allah s.w.t. by taking another wife (while his intentions are not my business)? Is that reason enough for me to rock the loving relationship I have with Allah s.w.t.? If I were to remarry, will I divorce every spouse who takes another wife, or would it not be hypocritical of me to remarry an already married man?

Ultimately, I agreed that my standing before Allah s.w.t. comes first, because as much as I fall short multiple times, I have this great urge to do actions to please Allah s.w.t.

The sweetest thing about my decision to stay was my firm faith that, if my leaving was for any reason other than my dislike for polygamy, then Allah s.w.t. would suffice even from places I never imagined as He promised in *Suratul Ṭalaq*:

"And We will provide for him from where he does not expect. And whoever relies upon Allah—then He is sufficient for him. Indeed, Allah will accomplish His purpose. Allah has already set for everything a [decreed] extent."

(at-Ṭalaq, 65:3)

I made *istikharah* (prayer for seeking counsel and guidance) on my decision to stay, and despite the ups and many downs, I am looking to Allah s.w.t. for compensation.

So, if there are issues with your marriage other than polygamy, then try and resolve them. Remember, if you have been able to successfully apply patience this far, ask yourself, if you could have some more patience, and if yes, *Alḥamdulillāh*, you will earn your reward, and if not, make consultation, then *istikharah* on your decision.

And if you just cannot accept living in polygamy, then remember Allah s.w.t. has not burdened a soul more than it can bear, and also make *istikharah* on your decision.

Please do not feel pressured to make a decision, even though your family and the society have their norms, but it is your life, an *amanah* (responsibility) between your Creator, Allah s.w.t. and you. And know that Allah s.w.t. never leaves any of His servants alone.

And remember with certainty, if you make whatever choice sincerely with Allah s.w.t. in mind, then Allah s.w.t is always enough for His striving servants.

Chapter Seven:

YOU SHOULD KNOW YOUR RIGHTS AND RESPONSIBILITIES

Islam has enjoined upon the husband duties towards his wife, and vice versa. *Insha'Allāh*, knowing these rights and understanding them will only open your heart more to the love Allah has for His creatures.

Please consider, no, I insist, that you get a concise book on the rights and responsibilities of Muslim spouses in marriage, and what I tried to do here is a summary, with citations from the Qur'an, *insha'Allāh*, but I could never do justice to this topic in this chapter, unlike a book.

Here are my highlights:

1. Financial rights; these are the monetary expectations from the husband. This could be:

    •   The *mahr* (dowry): This is the money to which the wife is entitled from her husband when the marriage contract is completed or when the marriage is consummated. It is a right which the man is obliged to pay to the woman.

    Allah s.w.t. says:

    "And give to the women (whom you marry) their *mahr* (obligatory bridal-money given by the husband to his wife at the time of marriage) with a good heart."

(an-Nisa', 4:4)

- Spending: The scholars of Islam agreed that it is obligatory for husbands to spend on their wives, on the condition that the wife makes herself available to her husband. If she refuses him or rebels, then she is not entitled to that spending. Spending on the women is also supported by a *hadith* on the Prophet Muḥammad s.a.w.'s Farewell Sermon:

Narrated from Jabir that the Messenger of Allah s.a.w. said in his Farewell Sermon:

"Fear Allah concerning women! Verily you have taken them on the security of Allah, and intercourse with them has been made lawful unto you by words of Allah. You too have rights over them, and that they should not allow anyone to sit on your bed [i.e., not let them into the house] whom you do not like. But if they do that, you can chastise them but not severely. Their rights upon you are that you should provide them with food and clothing in a fitting manner"

(Ṣaḥiḥ Muslim Book 15, Ḥadith 159)

- Accommodation: The husband should prepare for the wife's accommodation. This grants women their right to their private lodging, especially in a polygamous system. It allows women the freedom to thrive without resentment or feelings of jealousy, unlike when they have to live close to the other wives.

Allah s.w.t. says:

"Lodge them where you dwell, according to your means"

(at-Ṭalaq, 65:6)

2. The non-financial rights are:
- Fair treatment of co-wives: One of the rights that a wife has over her husband is that she and her co-wives should be treated equally if the husband has other wives. This is with regard to nights spent with them, spending, and clothing.

- Kind treatment: The husband must have a good attitude towards his wife and be kind to her, and offer her everything that may soften her heart towards him because Allah s.w.t. says:

> "...and live with them honorably"
>
> (an-Nisa', 4:19)

- Not harming one's wife: This is because harming others is ḥaram in the case of strangers, it is even more so in the case of harming one's wife. May Allah s.w.t. protect us all from harm.

To balance out our brief education on spousal rights, let me also highlight Allah's expectations of women in regard to their spouse—our responsibilities.

- The obligation of obedience to the husband is the responsibility of women, as long as their instructions are not against the command of Allah s.w.t. He has made the man a *qawwam* (protector and maintainer) of the woman, directing and taking care of her, by virtue of the physical faculties and the financial obligations that He has enjoined upon them.

Allah s.w.t. says:

"Men are the protectors and maintainers of women, because Allah has made one of them to excel the other, and because they spend (to support them) from their means"

(an-Nisa', 4:34)

• Wives should make themselves available to their husbands. One of the rights that the husband has over his wife is that he should be able to enjoy her (physically). Denying him of this right without a valid excuse is sinful.

Narrated that Abu Hurayrah r.a. said:

"The Messenger of Allah s.a.w. said: 'When a man calls his wife to his bed and she refuses, and he goes to sleep angry with her, the angels will curse her until morning.'

(Ṣaḥiḥ al-Bukhari, Book 59 Ḥadith 48)

• Another responsibility of the wife is that she should not permit anyone whom the husband dislikes to enter his house, even if that person is a close relation of hers.

Narrated from Abu Hurayrah r.a. that the Messenger of Allah s.a.w. said:

"It is not permitted for a woman to fast when her husband is present without his permission, or to admit anyone into his house without his permission. And whatever she spends (in charity) of his wealth without his consent..."

(Ṣaḥiḥ al-Bukhari, Book 67 Ḥadith 129)

• A wife should not be going out of the house except with the husband's permission, irrespective of the destination.

• Finally, the wife should treat her husband in a good manner, because Allah s.a.w. says:

"And they (women) have rights (over their husbands as regards living expenses) similar (to those of their husbands) over them (as regards obedience and respect) to what is reasonable."

(al-Baqarah, 2:228)

As I said earlier, this is an attempt to summarise the Muslim wife's rights and responsibilities, please consider reading dedicated texts on this topic for better appreciation.

Chapter Eight:

LISTING THE WORST-CASE SCENARIOS HELPS YOU CONQUER YOUR FEARS

This chapter kind of personalises this discussion. It will be you addressing your unique situation of polygamy, *insha'Allāh*, with a guide I used myself.

The worst-case scenario is a factual list I made through pessimistic lenses, documenting my deepest perceived fears against the worst possible outcomes. Making this list, cleared my head. Instead of the raging storm of 'what ifs' plaguing my brain, it reminded me that it was of course Allah s.w.t. who is in control.

For every terrible outcome my fears cooked up, the answer was always Allah s.w.t. Let me highlight:

The most fears that threaten women when faced with polygamy are:

- Fear of inadequacy

- Fear that the spouse will love them less

- Fear of being abandoned by a spouse

- Fear that the kids will not get their provisions

Well, those were my fears, and I created my pessimistic worst-outcome possible list:

- I am a totally useless person.

- My spouse goes away forever with the new wife, abandoning me and my kids.

- I am left broke, helpless with three dependents on the streets.

You must think I am wacko, right? Well, I had to state the fears, expand them out of proportion into a big scary monster, and then conquer it, *insha'Allāh*. And all the answers to my worries were the same thing:

- Isn't Allah, the Exalter, who can reward my striving, and grant me the honour?

- Isn't Allah, the Bestower, the Provider, the Rich, the Self-sufficient, who can supply my every need?

I kept the MP3 file of the ninety-nine names of Allah s.w.t. playing on repeat. I found the answer to all of my life questions in one place, *alḥamdulillāh*.

Isn't it absolutely sweet that we get to go to only one source for our every need? The Lord, the Friend, the Patron, the Forgiver, the Provider, the Cherisher, the Designer, the Comforter, the Giver and Taker and many more, all from the same source—Allah.

By Allah s.w.t., whenever I am troubled, I listen to His ninety-nine names, reflecting on their meanings, and my heart dares not to falter, moan, or fear afterwards.

I had only one fist for the monster I created:

"Allah is Sufficient for me, none has the right to be worshipped except Him, upon Him I rely, and He is Lord of the exalted throne."

(at-Tawbah, 9:129)

It became my mantra, it sufficed me, and it will suffice you.

Get your journal now. If you have not been journaling, please start today. It documents your yesterdays and acts as a proof for your tomorrow, that you grew today. Write your fears (no matter how insignificant), weave them into a huge monster of outcomes, then jam it with one fist, because really, is there any other answer than "The Fist".

Please note that this is an activity that you might have to do frequently because as Muslims our *iman* (faith) fluctuates. When you experience a 'high-*iman*' you want to go hang out with the other wife and braid each other's hair, and when the 'low-*iman*' sets in, you just want to bawl your eyes out while lying all day in bed.

Most times, these low feelings are responses to certain triggers, so note your triggers and avoid them if you can.

One of my triggers is actually when my spouse tries to complain about the challenges of maintaining multiple families—challenges I pointed out at first. There is this ringing in my ears that makes me want to wail and knock him silly with a heavy dose of "I told you", but since I am a slave of Allah s.w.t. striving for a high character and to please Him, I smile at him, remind him that Allah s.w.t. tries those He loves in different ways, and advise him to be patient. Suppressing my natural response to please Allah s.w.t. drains me, I feel weak, especially when I had a vast choice of words to choose from to rant against my spouse, and I really have to go back to the book of Allah s.w.t. to remind myself that I am strong and Allah s.w.t. loves the patient, not the quarrelsome.

So, you need to re-boost very frequently, especially, and immediately when you notice a downward slide in your *iman*. Please, do not wait until you crumble. And surround yourself, if available, with people who would reaffirm and strengthen your faith, not discourage you. If no one around you is enjoining patience and gratitude, it might be best that you keep to yourself.

This is a good time to count all of your many blessings, even if you will never number them. Then you will see how Allah s.w.t. has been so good to you!

Do you fear that after you have sacrificed your will to be free from this situation, He will leave you to yourself? No, Allah s.w.t. will never leave you to yourself, His word is binding, and His promise is true.

Polygamy, especially in a close-quarter living system, has its challenges. Even the mothers of the believers and the prophet's s.a.w. wives had misunderstandings, but with the guidance of Allah s.w.t., they were contained and not blown into fights.

Remember that just as you have misunderstandings with your sisters back at your parent's house, there will be issues here too, but the fear of Allah s.w.t. will keep our actions and words in check.

And if you want to live in separate quarters, Islam has given you the right to that. In fact, I am for separate quarters, separate houses, separate cities, and even separate countries if possible. So, take advantage of this right and avoid being nosy, do not concern yourself with what Allah s.w.t. has shielded you from!

Chapter Nine:

FOCUS IS PARAMOUNT

Allah s.w.t., our Creator and Sustainer says:

"And I have not created man, and jinn except for my worship"

(adh-Dhariyat, 51:56)

Our reason for existing is for the worship of Allah s.w.t. alone. All these other things we have, these things which distract us from our worship, these things which excite us so that our *salah* (prayer) is hasty or depresses us so we cannot find the willpower for worship, all of them are distractions of *dunya*—your spouse, your kids, the lovely home, and tasty food. They can be blessings if they help in your worship, or otherwise—if they turn you away from your worship to Allah s.w.t.

Look at the lives of the prophets, the *sahabah* (companions). Reflect on how they lived their lives.

Does love for their spouse and children disturb their love for Allah s.w.t.? Do we see them attached to a spouse so that they do not want to do good for the religion?

Look at their lives, see the striving, the migrations; do you think people who were attached to people or places could achieve so much?

By all means love your spouse, the Prophet s.a.w. loved his wives but do not ever let your love or attachments precede Allah's command. This is a great *jihad* (struggle) with the soul, especially for us in this Disney's *A Prince and a Princess* age, but it is a *jihad* worth fighting for.

Leaving all our worldly attachments allows us to focus on our essence of creation, which is Allah s.w.t. Know Him, know His beautiful names and recite His glorious book—He sent it down just for you.

Fall in love with Allah s.w.t., and let Him, the Loving, love you back.

One of the greatest gifts is knowing Allah s.w.t. through His ninety-nine names. Allow me to earn rewards for reintroducing you to them:

AR-RAḤMĀN The Most or Entirely Merciful

AR-RAḤĪM The Bestower of Mercy

AL-MĀLIK The King and Owner of Dominion

AL-QUDDŪS The Absolutely Pure

AS-SALĀM The Perfection and Giver of Peace

AL-MU'MIN The Faithful

AL-MUHAYMIN The Guardian

AL-'AZĪZ The All-Mighty

AL-JABBĀR The Compeller

AL-MUTAKABBIR The Supreme

AL-KHĀLIQ The Creator

AL-BĀRI' The Originator, The Evolver

AL-MUṢAWWIR The Bestower of Forms

AL-GHAFFĀR The All-Forgiving

AL-QAHHĀR The Subduer

AL-WAHHĀB The Giver of Gifts

AR-RAZZĀQ The Provider

AL-FATTĀḤ The Opener, The Judge

AL-ʿALĪM The All-Knowing

AL-QĀBIḌ The Withholder

AL-BĀSIṬ The Extender

AL-KHĀFIḌ The Abaser

AR-RĀFIʿ The Exalter

AL-MUʿIZZ The Giver of Honour

AL-MUDHIL The Giver of Dishonour

AS-SAMĪʿ The All-Hearing

AL-BAṢĪR The All-Seeing

AL-ḤAKAM The Judge

AL-ʿADL The Utterly Just

AL-LAṬĪF The Most Gentle

AL-KHABĪR The All-Aware

AL-ḤALĪM The Forbearing

AL-ʿAẒĪM The Magnificent

AL-GHAFŪR The Exceedingly Forgiving

ASH-SHAKŪR The Most Appreciative

AL-ʿALĪ The Most High

AL-KABĪR The Greatest

AL-ḤAFĪẒ The Preserver

AL-MUQĪT The Sustainer

AL-ḤASĪB The Sufficient

AL-JALĪL The Majestic

AL-KARĪM The Most Generous

AR-RAQĪB The Watchful

AL-MUJĪB The Responsive One

AL-WĀSIʿ The All-Encompassing

AL-ḤAKĪM The All-Wise

AL-WADŪD The Most Loving

AL-MAJĪD The Glorious

AL-BĀʿITH The Resurrector

ASH-SHAHĪD The Ever-Witnessing

AL-ḤAQQ The Absolute Truth

AL-WAKĪL The Disposer of Affairs

AL-QAWIYY The All-Strong

AL-MATĪN The Firm

AL-WALIYY The Protecting Friend

AL-ḤAMĪD The Praiseworthy

AL-MUḤṢĪ The Accounter

AL-MUBDI' The Originator

AL-MUʿĪD The Restorer

AL-MUḤYI The Giver of Life

AL-MUMĪT The Bringer of Death

AL-ḤAYY The Ever-Living

AL-QAYYŪM The Subsisting

AL-WĀJID The Perceiver

AL-MĀJID The Illustrious

AL-WĀḤID The One

AL-ĀḤAD The Unique

AṢ-ṢAMAD The Eternal, Satisfier of Needs

AL-QĀDIR The Capable, The Powerful

AL-MUQTADIR The Omnipotent

AL-MUQADDIM The Expediter

AL-MU'AKHKHIR The Delayer

AL-ʾAWWAL The First

AL-ʾĀKHIR The Last

AẒ-ẒĀHIR The Manifest

AL-BĀṬIN The Hidden One, Knower of the Hidden

AL-WĀLĪ The Patron

AL-MUTAʿĀLĪ The Supremely Exalted

AL-BARR The Good

AT-TAWWĀB The Ever-Relenting

AL-MUNTAQIM The Avenger

AL-ʿAFŪW The Pardoner

AR-RAʾŪF The Most Kind

MĀLIKUL-MULK Master of the Kingdom, Owner of the Dominion

DHUL-JALĀLI WAL-IKRĀM Possessor of Glory and Honour, Lord of Majesty and Generosity

AL-MUQSIṬ The Requiter

AL-JĀMIʿ The Gatherer, The Uniter

AL-GHANĪ The Self-Sufficient, The Wealthy

AL-MUGHNĪ The Enricher

AL-MĀNI' The Withholder

AD-DĀRR The Distressor

AN-NĀFI' The Benefactor

AN-NŪR The Light

AL-HĀDĪ The Guide

AL-BADĪ' The Incomparable, The Originator

AL-BĀQĪ The Everlasting

AL-WĀRITH The Inheritor of All

AR-RASHĪD The Guide to the Right Path

AS-SABŪR The Patient One

Imagine our Lord, Allah s.w.t. with these beautiful names. Is there any possible situation that any one of these names does not suffice?

Whenever I am disturbed, I ponder on the names of Allah s.w.t., then I choose the name that applies to my worries, and I go to Allah s.w.t. in *sajdah* (prostration), calling Him by these beautiful names.

When I am broke, it is *Ya Mughniyy*, the Enricher, please enrich me, *Ya Razzāq*, the Provider, please provide for me.

When my heart feels dark, dead, far from Allah s.w.t., I call on *al-Muhyī*, and He responds.

When I feel alone, *al-Waliyy*, the Protecting Friend, is always near me.

There is no situation whatsoever that Allah s.w.t. has not covered. When I am distressed, at times I listen to my MP3 file of the names of Allah s.w.t., and if my heart does not calm quickly, I say to it:

"Oh heart, I dare you not to find solace in Allah s.w.t. Who created you, and Who encompasses all things."

My heart quickly realigns itself, and by the aid of Allah s.w.t., it works every time.

I have used basic translations for the names of Allah s.w.t., in clear-spaced out texts, to help you grasp its blessings even if you only skimmed over them.

CONCLUSION

All praises and thanks to the Lord of the
worlds, Allah s.w.t. He alone could have
guided me here. May He make this work
beneficial by His mercy. *Amīn.*

www.ingramcontent.com/pod-product-compliance
Lightning Source LLC
Chambersburg PA
CBHW061300140726
47998CB00006B/2296